FROM TRASH TO TREASURE

# HOLIDAY CRAFTS

by Gini Holland

**PowerKiDS** press

New York

Published in 2014 by The Rosen Publishing Group, Inc.
29 East 21st Street, New York, NY 10010

First Edition

Produced for Rosen by Ruby Tuesday Books Ltd
Editor for Ruby Tuesday Books Ltd: Mark J. Sachner
US Editor: Kara Murray
Designer: Emma Randall

Photo Credits:
Cover, 1, 3, 4–5, 6, 14–15, 16–17, 18–19, 22, 30–31 © Shutterstock; cover, 1, 6–7, 8–9, 10–11, 12–13, 20–21, 22–23, 24–25, 26–27, 28–29, 30–31 © Ruth Owen and John Such.

Library of Congress Cataloging-in-Publication Data

Holland, Gini.
 Holiday crafts / by Gini Holland. — First edition.
    pages cm. — (From trash to treasure)
 Includes index.
 ISBN 978-1-4777-1286-3 (library binding) — ISBN 978-1-4777-1366-2 (pbk.) — ISBN 978-1-4777-1367-9 (6-pack)
 1. Holiday decorations—Juvenile literature. 2. Handicraft—Juvenile literature. I. Title.
 TT900.H6H67 2014
 745.594'1—dc23

                                2012047078

Manufactured in the United States of America

CPSIA Compliance Information: Batch #S13PK8: For Further Information contact Rosen Publishing, New York, New York at 1-800-237-9932

# CONTENTS

# CELEBRATE YOUR HOLIDAY TRASH

Each year, people celebrate holidays by making decorations, sending cards, wrapping presents, eating special treats, and spending time with friends and family.

People have a lot of fun, but they also use a lot of the Earth's **resources**. In fact, each year, the number of Christmas cards sold to Americans could fill a building that is 10 stories tall and covers as much ground as a football field!

So, this year, why not make your decorations from **recycled** materials? That way, you can have fun and still protect the Earth and its many resources. This book contains six craft projects that use materials such as newspaper, recycled ribbon and cards, and even old CDs. You'll be helping the **environment** while you enjoy the holidays, from autumn right through until spring. Now, that's something to celebrate!

Half the paper used in the United States goes to wrap and decorate presents.

How many greetings cards does your family send and throw away each year?

If each American family reused 2 feet (0.6 m) of unused or leftover ribbon, it would be enough ribbon to wrap around the entire planet!

When did you last throw away a CD or DVD?

# SODA BOTTLE HALLOWEEN GHOSTS

Every hour of every day, around 2.5 million plastic bottles are used in the United States. The bottles might contain shampoo, cleaning products, or drinks such as water and soda.

Soda bottles can be recycled and the plastic made into new bottles and other products such as fleece jackets and even carpets! It's also possible for you to give a soda bottle an extra life by reusing it before you recycle it.

This Halloween, stores will be filled with newly-made, plastic decorations, but why not make your own? Using large soda bottles, pre-used black cardboard or paper, and some white fabric from an old unwanted sheet or pair of curtains, you can create these easy-to-make ghost lamps.

## You will need:

- An empty 2-liter soda bottle for each ghost
- A craft knife
- Two pieces of thin white fabric, such as cheesecloth, muslin, or net, each measuring approximately 24 inches x 24 inches (60 cm x 60 cm)
- Elmer's glue (mixed three parts glue to one part water)
- A paintbrush
- Pre-used black cardboard or thick paper
- Scissors
- An LED tealight or small flashlight

## STEP 1:

Ask an adult to help you cut off the top section of the empty soda bottle with the craft knife.

cut here

## STEP 2:
For each ghost, cut two eyes and a mouth from the black cardboard or paper.

24 inches (60 cm)

## STEP 3:
Take the two pieces of fabric and cut a large circle from each.

Brush glue here

## STEP 4:
Brush some glue into the center of one of the fabric circles with the paintbrush.

## STEP 5:

Place the soda bottle bottom up and then drape the fabric circle over the bottle, glue side down. The area where you brushed the glue should be pressed onto the bottom of the bottle.

## STEP 6:

The thin fabric will be sticky and wet with glue, so as it drapes over the ghost's "head" you can pleat or slightly crumple it to create the folds of your ghost's "body."

## STEP 7:

Now, repeat steps 4, 5, and 6 with the second fabric circle.

## STEP 8:

Glue black eyes and a mouth to the ghost's head.

## STEP 9:

Finally, stand the ghost over an LED tealight and arrange the folds of its body to make a spooky, ghostly shape.

# THANKSGIVING TABLE-TOP TURKEY

A real turkey cooks in two to four hours, depending on its size. But you'll need three to four days to create this **papier-mâché** turkey decoration. It will be worth it, though!

The great thing about papier-mâché is that its main ingredient is newspaper. Every newspaper that comes into your home has required **energy** in the **manufacturing** process. It may also have used as much as 79 gallons (300 l) of water to produce it.

Newspapers are a product that piles up in homes and **landfills** daily, but thankfully, Americans recycle more than 60 percent of the newspapers they buy. This helps stop forests from being cut down to make more paper and keeps landfills from piling even higher. You can also do your part for the Earth by reusing a newspaper this Thanksgiving to make a fun decoration.

## You will need:

- A newspaper
- Extra newspaper to protect your table or countertop
- Two balloons
- Cooking oil
- Elmer's glue (mixed three parts glue to one part water)
- A paintbrush
- Black marker
- A craft knife
- A toilet paper tube
- Three cups of dry sand or pebbles
- Tape
- White and brown paint
- Cardboard in various colors and patterns
- Scissors
- A glue gun
- Googly eyes
- A small piece of red fabric or felt

**STEP 1:**
Tear the newspaper into strips about 1 inch (2.5 cm) wide.

**STEP 2:**
Blow up the balloons so one is about 10 inches (25 cm) long and one is about 5 inches (12.5 cm) long.

**STEP 3:**
Smear the balloons with cooking oil. This will keep the papier-mâché from sticking to the balloon when it is dry.

**STEP 4**:

Using the paintbrush, brush some of the glue mixture onto the side of the large balloon. Lay a strip of newspaper onto the glue, and then brush more glue over the top. Repeat this with more newspaper strips, slightly overlapping each strip, until the balloon is covered and only the knot can be seen.

**STEP 5**:

Repeat step 4 on the small balloon. Then, allow the papier-mâché to dry for 24 hours.

**STEP 6**:

Add a second layer of newspaper strips to each balloon and allow to dry for 24 hours. Then add a third layer and allow to dry for 24 hours.

**STEP 7**:

Place the end of the toilet paper tube over the knotted end of the large balloon. Trace a circle onto the papier-mâché. Repeat for the small balloon. Cut out the two circles, popping and pulling out the balloons.

**STEP 8**:

Pour the sand or pebbles into the turkey's body so it stands up by itself.

**STEP 9**:

Use the toilet paper tube as a neck to join the body to the head and tape in place. Then cover the neck and tape with a layer of papier-mâché.

**STEP 10:**
Paint the turkey white to cover all the newspaper. When dry, paint the turkey brown.

**STEP 11:**
Cut tail feathers and wings from colorful cardboard.

Tail feathers

Wings

**STEP 12:**
Make a cone-shaped beak from a small piece of thick paper or cardboard. Cut a long, thin teardrop shape from the red fabric to make the turkey's snood.

Cardboard tail feathers

Snood

Cardboard wing

**STEP 13:**
When the paint is dry, use the glue gun to stick on the tail feathers, wings, beak, snood, and googly eyes. Your turkey is ready to gobble-gobble!

# CD ORNAMENTS

When your old CD or DVD just skips and stutters, it's time to put it in the recycling bin. However, it's a "number 7" plastic, which means you can't just put it in your own recycling bin.

Most communities will not take this kind of plastic for recycling. In fact, billions of CDs and DVDs are made each year, and millions of these discs get tossed into landfills or get burned in **incinerators**. Burning plastic puts unwanted chemicals into the air we breathe.

To recycle a disc properly, you should go online and find a local place that will take it. Or you could turn it into a holiday decoration for Christmas, Hanukkah, or Kwanzaa, and enjoy it for years to come.

## You will need:

- A used CD or DVD (for each decoration)
- A glue gun
- Paint (suitable for use on plastic)
- A paintbrush
- Buttons and beads from old clothes or pieces of jewelry
- About 6 inches (15 cm) of reused ribbon, yarn, or string to hang each ornament
- Pre-used gift bows
- Scissors

**STEP 1:**

Trim pretty buttons from old pieces of unwanted clothing, or take apart old or broken bracelets and necklaces.

**STEP 2:**

If the disk has pictures or writing on one side, paint this side in a bright color. You can paint both sides of the CD, if you wish, or leave the shiny side its original color. Allow the paint to dry.

**STEP 3:**

Using the glue gun, put a small spot of glue onto the disc. Then, carefully drop a bead or button onto the glue, taking care not to touch the hot glue with your fingers.

**STEP 4:**

Be as creative as you like with your designs!

**WARNING**
Only use a glue gun if an adult is there to help you.

**STEP 5:**
When you have finished adding decorations to your disc, allow the glue to dry and cool.

**STEP 6:**
Finally thread a piece of ribbon, string, or yarn through the center of the disc. Alternatively, glue a piece of ribbon, string, or yarn to one side of the disc.

# PEACE AND FREEDOM BELL

To honor Dr. King on Martin Luther King Jr. Day, make a bell with black and white hand shapes that clap for peace and freedom.

Help the planet by making your decoration from a plastic yogurt or drink container, scrap cardboard, and used aluminum foil.

By reusing a plastic container, you make sure it does not end up in a landfill, or worse. For example, the Arctic Ocean has twice as much plastic and trash littering its seabed as it did ten years ago. A lot of this trash is dumped by fishing boats and other ships. Sea animals are getting tangled in plastic bags and pushed from their homes on the seafloor by plastic and other junk.

As Dr. King once said, "The time is always right to do what is right." So what are you waiting for? Reuse that plastic container, and help protect the planet!

## You will need:

- White and black cardboard
- A pencil
- Scissors
- Colorful paints
- A paintbrush
- A large yogurt or drink container
- Recycled, clean aluminum foil (washed and dried if needed)
- A length of ribbon, string, or yarn

**STEP 1:**

Place your hand on the white cardboard and draw around it with a pencil to make a hand silhouette. Repeat on the black cardboard.

**STEP 2:**

Cut out both hand shapes.

**STEP 3:**
Paint the word "Peace" on both sides of one hand. Paint "Freedom" in the same way on the other hand.

**STEP 4:**
Pierce a hole in the wrist end of each hand with scissors.

**STEP 5:**
Pierce a hole in the bottom of the container with the scissors. Rotate the scissors to make the hole round.

**STEP 6:**
Cover the container with aluminum foil. Pierce the foil where it covers the hole in the container.

**STEP 7:**

Thread a ribbon through each wrist hole of your cardboard hands and knot the ribbon.

**STEP 8:**

Thread the strings up through the bell and out the hole. Knot the strings above the bell, making sure the hands hang at the height you want beneath the bell.

**STEP 9:**

Hang your bell from a curtain rod, door wreath hook, doorknob, or other hook. Let peace and freedom ring!

# ORIGAMI VALENTINE'S CARD

Valentine's Day means hearts, flowers, candy, and cards. Around the world, each year, people give close to one billion Valentine's cards to one another. That's a lot of love. It's also a lot of paper!

You can help save some of that paper by recycling cardboard and pieces of gift wrap and using them to make cards. You will also save a little bit of the tree that went into making the paper.

Cut **origami** squares from gently used gift wrap or colored paper, and you will be able to fold them into one-of-a kind hearts to decorate a handmade Valentine's card.
Look for paper that's red, pink, purple, or a mix of these colors. Fold the paper into this special shape and show some love to a favorite person. He or she will thank you, and so will planet Earth.

## You will need:

- A piece of cardboard or thick paper (to make the card)
- Pieces of colorful used paper or gift wrap
- Scissors
- Glue
- Marker or colored pen

**STEP 1:**
To make a heart, cut a piece of colored paper or gift wrap into a square that measures 6 inches x 6 inches (15 cm x 15 cm).

**STEP 2:**
Place the paper colored side down. Fold along the dotted lines and crease.

**STEP 3:**
Fold down the top point to meet the center, and crease.

**STEP 4:**
Fold up the bottom point to meet the top of the model, and crease.

**STEP 5:**
Fold in the right side along the dotted line so it lines up with the center of the model, and crease.

**STEP 6:**
Now fold the left side into the center so the two sides meet, and crease.

A          B

**STEP 7:**
Turn the model over and fold in points A and B. Crease well.

**STEP 8:**
Now fold down points C and D, and crease well.

**STEP 9:**
Turn the model over and your origami heart is complete!

**STEP 10:**
Make two or three hearts and then use them to decorate a handmade Valentine's card.

**STEP 11:**
Make your card by folding a colorful piece of cardboard or thick paper in half. Then glue on your origami hearts and, if you wish, write a Valentine's message.

Happy Valentine's Day

**STEP 12:**
In early February, keep watch for any boxes or packaging that contains colorful materials. You can use these recycled materials to make your card.

# LOOPY SPRING BASKETS

Your old sweater has kept you warm all winter, but now it has holes in the elbows. Its cuffs are frayed. It's getting too small for you to wear next year, and it really is too worn-out to give away. Should you toss it?

No, wait! How about pulling out the yarn? If you pull a yarn end from one row of stitches, you will be able to pull your sweater apart, stitch by stitch. Roll the yarn into a ball as you go. Alternatively ask around if people have any scraps of yarn they are planning to throw away that you can recycle.

Use the recycled yarn to make this simple and colorful basket that's perfect for holding Easter eggs and other treats.

## You will need:

- A ceramic or plastic bowl
- Recycled yarn in one or more spring colors
- Scissors
- Plastic wrap
- Elmer's glue
  (mixed three parts glue to one part water)

## STEP 1:

Choose a ceramic or plastic bowl that will be the form, or shape, for your yarn basket.

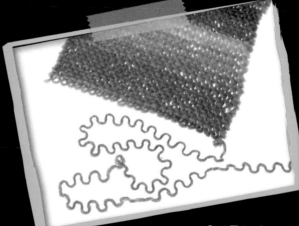
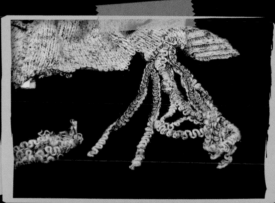

## STEP 2:

Pick apart and unravel old woolen items or gather yarn scraps.

## STEP 3:

Cut the yarn into 17-inch (43 cm) long strands. You will need enough to cover the outside of the bowl.

**STEP 4**:
Cover the bowl with plastic wrap.

**STEP 5**:
Soak the yarn in the glue and water mix.

**STEP 6**:
Pull a strand of yarn from the glue, stripping off excess glue with your fingers, and loop and drape it over your bowl.

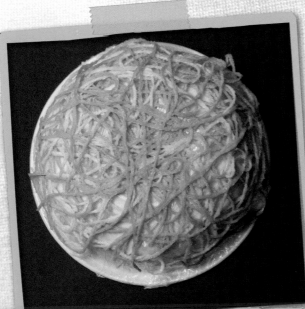

**STEP 7**:
Overlap the yarn in loops until the bowl is fully but lightly covered. Some holes between strands of yarn will give your bowl a lacy effect.

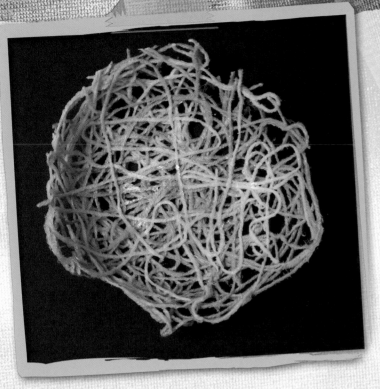

**STEP 8:**
Let the yarn dry overnight. By morning, the yarn will have dried and set hard.

**STEP 9:**
Gently pull the yarn basket from the bowl, and your loopy basket is ready to fill with treats!

# GLOSSARY

**energy** (EH-ner-jee)
The ability to do work.

**environment**
(en-VY-ern-ment)
The area where plants and
animals live, along with all the
things, such as weather, that
affect that area; often used to
describe the natural world.

**incinerators**
(in-SIH-nuh-ray-turz)
Furnaces used to burn waste
materials, including plastics
and other materials that do not
decompose or rot, at very high
temperatures until they are
reduced to ash.

**landfills** (LAND-filz)
Large sites where garbage is
dumped and buried.

**manufacturing**
(man-yuk-FAK-cher-ing)
Making a product on a large
scale, usually using machines.

**origami** (or-uh-GAH-mee)
The art of folding paper into
decorative shapes or objects.

**papier-mâché** (pay-per-mah-SHAY)
A material made from newspapers and glue that can be molded when it is wet. It hardens as it dries, so it can be used for making models and sculptures.

**recycled** (ree-SY-kuld)
Having to do with used materials turned into new products.

**resources** (REE-sawrs-ez)
Materials or substances that occur in nature such as wood, rocks, and water.

# WEBSITES

Due to the changing nature of Internet links, PowerKids Press has developed an online list of websites related to the subject of this book. This site is updated regularly. Please use this link to access the list:

www.powerkidslinks.com/ftt/holi/

# READ MORE

**Gnojewski, Carol**. *St. Patrick's Day Crafts*. Berkeley Heights, NJ: Enslow Publishers, Inc. 2004.

**Lynette, Rachel**. *Let's Throw a Valentine's Day Party!* New York, NY: The Rosen Publishing Group, 2012.

**Umnik, Sharon Dunn**. *Easy-to-Do Holiday Crafts from Everyday Household Items*. Honesdale, PA: Boyds Mills Press, 2005.

# INDEX